Making a Deal

Rob Waring, *Series Editor*

HEINLE
CENGAGE Learning

Australia • Brazil • Japan • Korea • Mexico • Singapore • Spain • United Kingdom • United States

Words to Know

This story is set in Northern Africa in the country of Morocco. It happens in the city of Fes [fɛz].

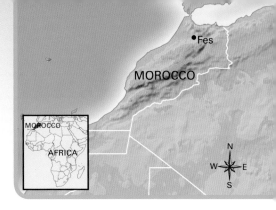

A **In the *Souk*.** Read the paragraph. Use the correct form of the underlined words to complete the definitions.

There are *souks* [suks] in most Middle Eastern and Arab cities. A *souk* is an ancient kind of market that is usually full of narrow alleys, or walkways. *Souks* have many stalls where people can buy things. They can buy beautiful jewelry to wear. They can also buy clothes, such as kaftans, as well as shoes and sandals. There are also craftsmen in the *souks* who make tables and other objects. If shoppers get hungry, they can get delicious local fruits, like dates, to eat.

1. attractive objects that people wear to look nice: _____

2. a small shop with an open front: _____

3. a narrow road between buildings: _____

4. someone who uses special skills to make things: _____

5. a sweet, sticky brown fruit: _____

6. a long piece of clothing: _____

7. a light, open shoe that is often worn in warm weather: _____

kaftan

dates

B **Making a Deal.** Read the paragraph. Then match each word or phrase with the correct definition.

   In the *souk*, there are usually no prices listed. People must bargain to decide upon a price. The vendor, or seller, usually starts by naming a price. Then, the buyer asks for a discount, or suggests a lower price. This goes on until the people make a deal and agree on an amount. They usually arrange to pay a final price that's between the vendor's first price and the buyer's discounted price. Most Moroccan people are very good at bargaining. Some people say that it's a game in Morocco, or even a national sport!

1. bargain _____

2. vendor _____

3. discount _____

4. make a deal _____

5. arrange _____

a. a lowering of a price; money off

b. reach an agreement, especially in business

c. a person who sells things

d. plan or agree to

e. discuss prices with somebody in order to agree on one price

sandals

jewelry

Stalls in the *Souk*

3

The *souk* in the city of Fes is Morocco's oldest market. It's an ancient shopping center that has a lot of narrow alleys that are crowded with shops and stalls. In one of these stalls, a craftsman is making patterns in the surface of a metal table top. But while he makes patterns, people all around him are making deals. This is business, Moroccan-style, and many people here in the *souk* are bargaining as hard as they can.

CD 3, Track 03

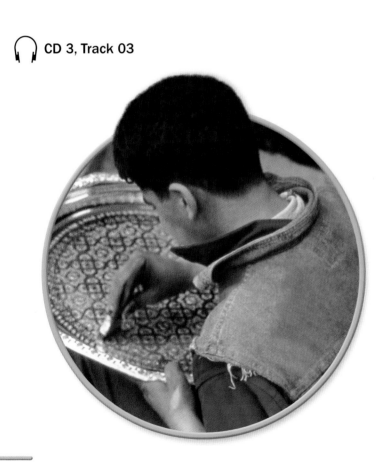

All the sales in the *souk* happen face-to-face; it's very personal and very busy! The vendors have everything a shopper could possibly want. There are sandals next to fish bowls, and nearby, birds in **cages**[1] watch the whole scene. One vendor sells kaftans, while his neighbor sells **slippers**.[2] Across the alley, a man sells dates and **apricots**[3] to hungry shoppers. In the *souk*, there really is something for everyone. In the city of Fes, a certain kind of small, red hat is also very easy to find. This famous hat, called the *fez*, was created here and named after the city.

---

[1]**cage:** a structure in which animals or birds are kept
[2]**slipper:** a soft, comfortable shoe usually worn in the house
[3]**apricot:** a small, soft orange fruit

bird cage

fish bowls

fez

slippers

apricots

The vendors in the souk have everything a shopper could want!

A visit to the *souk* is a lesson in Moroccan bargaining culture. For visitors, the question is not 'What should I buy?' but 'How should I buy it?' That's where they get a real education in making a deal.

Two Dutch tourists talk about what they have learned so far in the *souk*. "You have to start yourself at one third [of the original price] or something," the man says, "and then you bargain up to 50 percent." "Yeah," agrees his female friend, "and they go down [in price] twice as hard as we go up with the price! Then you get it at half the price they say at first." The man then adds, "But it's really a game. The Moroccans are very good at bargaining and they say they are the best in the world."

Ahmed Garib,[4] a Moroccan tour guide, explains why Moroccans are so good at bargaining. According to him, it's almost a way of life for them. "You know, here in Moroccan culture, for everything … you should bargain," he says. "We don't have [a] really fixed price."

In the *souk* in Fes, shopping is an exercise in bargaining. Here, it's the natural thing to do, and almost everyone does it. However, visitors who want to practice making a deal here had better be careful! They ought to know a few things before they begin.

---

[4] **Ahmed Garib:** [ɑkmɛd gɑɾ̞ib]

Predict

Answer 'True' or 'False'. Then, scan pages 13-18 to check your answers.

1. Beginners at bargaining always pay more.

2. Foreigners pay more than Moroccan people.

3. Vendors offer their customers tea.

4. Tourists never buy things that they don't really want.

Beginners at bargaining pay more. How much more? According to Ahmed, "Sometimes 20 to 30 percent more [than] the price that the Moroccan people pay." He then continues with some advice, "So you should always [bargain]. For example, if [the vendor] charges 1000 **dirham**,[5] you give him 600 dirham, then you go up, he go[es] down, and then you can arrange [it] between you."

The vendors of the *souk* are not trying to **cheat**[6] customers. It's more like a test to find out who is the best or the strongest bargainer. According to one jewelry seller, "Some customers pay more than [others]. We find customers [to be easier if] they don't bargain too much."

---

[5]**dirham:** Moroccan money; 1 U.S. dollar = about 8 dirham
[6]**cheat:** get money in an unfair manner; get an advantage with lies

The real test for any bargainer is the **carpet**[7] shop. This is where the sellers really pressure customers to buy something. On one particular afternoon, a carpet vendor is trying to sell a carpet to some tourists. He wants to get the best price for his carpet, and it seems that the buyer's first offer is far too low. "Excuse me," the salesman says, "you want to buy [a] **camel**[8] for the price of [a] **donkey**?"[9] He laughs, but then adds, "Impossible. That's too low, believe me, that's too low." As he continues laughing, he reaches for another carpet and proceeds to try to make a deal.

---

[7] **carpet:** a thick material used for covering floors
[8] **camel:** a large animal that lives in the desert and has one or two raised parts on its back
[9] **donkey:** an animal that looks like a small horse with long ears
Note: In Morocco and other Arab cultures, camels are often valued more than donkeys.

Carpet vendors can be one of the biggest tests for a shopper!

Sometimes, strong salesmen like these don't give up easily! One English tourist explains: "Once you end up in a shop, you sit there drinking tea, and you say 'I don't want to buy anything.' But then **he's like**,[10] 'Well, just offer a price … offer a price. 500? What's your best price?' And you're like, 'We don't want to buy it.' And they're like, 'Okay, 300!'"

This strong selling style is all part of the game. The carpet vendor explains the game of bargaining as he sees it: "Well we ask a little bit a high[er] price because everyone comes with an intention to bargain. They know that in Morocco they bargain a lot, so of course we leave a step to make discounts and **haggling over**[11] the price."

Some shoppers enjoy the bargaining challenge, too. One carpet shopper explains, "The secret is looking very careful[ly] at how [the sellers] do it. Watch them … [watch] how they move, and then go step by step, and see where you end."

---

[10]**(he's/you're/they're) like:** *(slang)* sometimes used for quoting speech (e.g. "He's like" = "He says")
[11]**haggle over (something):** bargain

There is one thing that all tourists should watch out for in the *souk*: they shouldn't buy too much! According to one Dutch tourist, it's sometimes difficult to leave things behind. "The thing is, they make it so cheap for you!" he says. "They start up so high, and at the end it sounds so cheap," he explains. "It's only one sixth of the price, or one eighth of the price. [So you say] 'Well, for this money, I can't leave it!'"

For some visitors to Fes, it may be difficult to leave without buying more than they planned. One thing here is certain—at the *souk*, everyone can make a deal!

TELEPHONE

What do you think?

1. Would it be easy for you to bargain in a *souk*?

2. Would you like to try it? Why or why not?

3. What would you buy at the *souk*?

After You Read

1. What's the main purpose of page 4?
   A. to introduce ancient shopping in Morocco
   B. to show people making deals
   C. to describe a *souk*
   D. to give an example of fast business

2. What market item was named for the city of Fes?
   A. slippers
   B. the kaftan
   C. sandals
   D. a hat

3. The *souk* teaches shoppers _____ bargain.
   A. to
   B. about
   C. by
   D. in

4. On page 9, what advice do the Dutch tourists give about bargaining?
   A. Bargain down to half price.
   B. Start with a high price.
   C. Start low and then go up.
   D. Get the price down to one third.

5. According to Ahmed Garib, why are Moroccans good at bargaining?
   A. because it's part of their culture
   B. because their prices are always fixed
   C. because they enjoy meeting tourists
   D. because they don't like using money

6. In paragraph 2 on page 10, 'it's' refers to:
   A. fixing a price
   B. bargaining
   C. selling
   D. shopping

7. Customers who pay more than others are generally
   _____ bargainers.
   A. unfair
   B. advanced
   C. efficient
   D. new

8. On page 14, to what is 'that's too low' referring?
   A. a carpet
   B. a camel
   C. an offer
   D. a donkey

9. What is the writer's purpose on page 14?
   A. to show that bargaining is like a game
   B. to show that carpet vendors are mean
   C. to show that tourists are weak bargainers
   D. to show someone buying an item

10. On page 17, what does the tourist actually want to buy?
    A. a carpet
    B. some tea
    C. a game
    D. nothing

11. Which is NOT a suitable heading for paragraph 3 on page 17?
    A. Shopper Enjoys a Challenge
    B. No Discounts Today
    C. Shopper Studies Sellers
    D. Go Step by Step

12. Why do some visitors buy more than they planned?
    A. because the deals are so good
    B. because tourists love to bargain
    C. because they have a lot of money
    D. because Fes is expensive

SAVE WHILE YOU SPEND

By Skip Stevens

A warm welcome to all of you first-year students! I hope you'll enjoy your years at Northfield College and that you'll benefit from the excellent education you'll get here. You already know that a good education is not cheap, so it's important for students to save money where they can. I've discovered some great strategies for finding bargains. My hints will save you money on college essentials, such as books, clothing, and furniture. Happy shopping!

Used Books

The Internet is a good place to find low prices on things you need, particularly books. Many sites have listings from individuals who are selling their own items. They sometimes also have listings from large companies. You can often buy books at a discount of 50 percent or more. You can also find books from countries all over the world. This is a great opportunity if you are studying foreign languages!

Freecycle

'Freecycle' is an organization that helps people give away things they don't need anymore. Everything is free! First, join the Freecycle group in your community. (There are over 4,000 groups worldwide.) Then, check the Freecycle listings to see what people are giving away. If you discover something you need, contact the person and arrange to pick up the item. It's a great alternative to regular shopping.

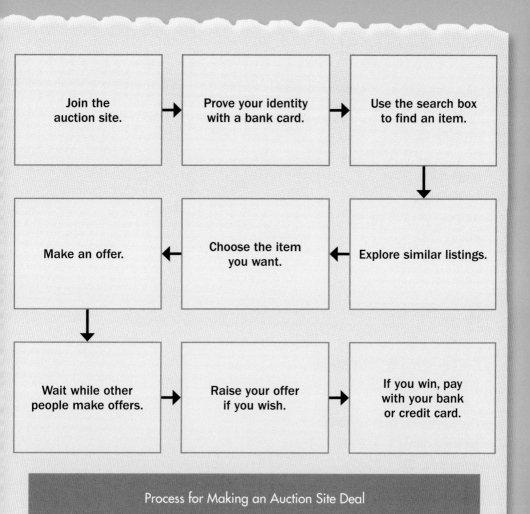

| Join the auction site. | → | Prove your identity with a bank card. | → | Use the search box to find an item. |

| Make an offer. | ← | Choose the item you want. | ← | Explore similar listings. |

| Wait while other people make offers. | → | Raise your offer if you wish. | → | If you win, pay with your bank or credit card. |

Process for Making an Auction Site Deal

Online Auctions

Some Internet sites allow you to make a deal for anything you need at a very low price. First, you have to become a member of the site. Then, you can shop for anything you want. You offer whatever you want to pay for an item. Then, if the seller agrees, it's yours! It's really easy to make deals on these sites. The chart shows how it works. Be careful to use only safe and secure websites!

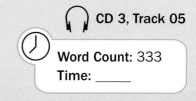

CD 3, Track 05

Word Count: 333
Time: _____

23

Vocabulary List

alley (2, 4, 6)
apricot (6, 7)
arrange (3, 13)
bargain (3, 9, 10, 11, 13, 14, 17, 19)
cage (6)
camel (14)
carpet (14, 15, 17)
cheat (13)
craftsman (2, 4)
date (2, 6)
dirham (13)
discount (3, 17)
donkey (14)
haggle over (something) (17)
jewelry (2, 13)
kaftan (2, 6)
(he's/you're/they're) like (17)
make a deal (3, 4, 9, 10, 14, 18)
sandal (2, 6)
slipper (6, 7)
stall (2, 4)
vendor (3, 6, 7, 11, 13, 14, 15, 17)